Adventures in Journaling

PAPER ADVENTURES

by Joanna Campbell Slan

Acknowledgements. A heartfelt thank you to the team at Paper Adventures for their support of my work.

Adventures in Journaling. Copyright © 2002, Joanna Campbell Slan. All rights reserved. This book may not be duplicated in any form without written permission from the publisher, except in the form of brief excerpts or quotations for the purposes of review.

First Edition. Printed and bound in the United States of America.
06 05 04 03 02   5 4 3 2 1
ISBN: 1-930500-09-2

Limit of Liability & Disclaimer. The author, publisher and sponsor have used their best efforts in preparing this book. The author, publisher and sponsor make no warranty of any kind, expressed or implied, with regard to the instructions and suggestions contained in this book. Due to inconsistent conditions, tools and individual skill level, the author, publisher and sponsor cannot be responsible for injuries, losses and/or other damages which may result from the use of the information in this book.

The snapshots featured in the scrapbook page layouts throughout this book are used with permission.

Trademarks. Diamond Dust™, Flannel Sheets™, Hot Potatoes™, Mix'n'Match Archivals™, Page Flippers™, Parchlucent™, PostScript Paper™, Quadrants™, Two-Tone Archivals™ and Velveteen Paper™ are trademarks of Paper Adventures. Paper Adventures® is a registered trademark of Paper Adventures.

Jill's Paper Doll World MatchMakers™ and Jill's Paper Doll World SceneMakers™ are trademarks of Jill Rinner. Dee-lightful Prints™ is trademark of Dee Gruenig.

k. p. kids & co.™ is a trademark of Kari Pearson.

PuzzleMates® is a registered trademark of PuzzleMates.

Scrapbook Storytelling® is a registered trademark of Joanna Campbell Slan.

Published by:
EFG, Inc.
St. Louis, MO
(314) 353-6100

Distributed to the trade markets by:
North Light Books
an imprint of F&W Publications, Inc.
4700 East Galbraith Road
Cincinnati, OH 45236
(800) 289-0963; fax (513) 531-4082

- and -

Paper Adventures
P.O. Box 04393
Milwaukee, WI 53204
(414) 383-0414; fax (414) 383-0760
www.paperadventures.com

Inside: An Adventure...

Jump-start your journey with easy pages

- ❏ Keepin' it Together 5
- ❏ Making Good Time 6
- ❏ Broad Stripes, Bright Stars 7
- ❏ A Match Made in Heaven 8
- ❏ Rough Rides, Easy Crops 9
- ❏ Take a Solid Swing 10
- ❏ Leafing the Country 11

Set the stage with textures and colors

- ❏ Foot-Tapping Textures 12
- ❏ Mouth-Watering Velveteen 13
- ❏ The Color of Love 14

Adventures in Journaling

Explore the possibilities of PostScript Paper

- Facing Pages, Facing Photos 15
- A Full Count with Photos 16
- A Parade of Possibilities 17
- Seeing Double-Stuff 18
- Find Your Thrill 19
- Journaling with PostScript Paper 20

Discover new ways to use great products

- Cap It Off with Journaling 31
- Whimsical Travels & Destinations 32
- The Spirit of Scrapbooking 33

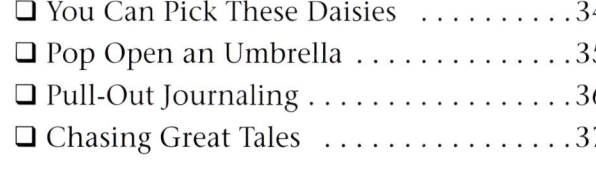

Add a visual P.S. to your scrapbook pages

- Bounce & Flip It 21
- A Storybook Wedding 22
- Egging on a Greeting 23
- A Place for All Senses 24
- Color in Harmony with Paper 25
- Jumping Up Geraniums 26
- Step-by-Step Storytelling 27

Pick up and go with interactive pages

- You Can Pick These Daisies 34
- Pop Open an Umbrella 35
- Pull-Out Journaling 36
- Chasing Great Tales 37

Pack in powerful images with paper

- Saving Stories of Our Times 38
- Cherry & Cheery Checks 39
- Teaming Up for Fun 40

Take your sparkling pages to The Ritz

- Star-Spangled Apple 28
- Jumping Into Sparkling Water 29
- Glamour in Glitter 30

Making Albums

- A Garden of Paper Delight 42

How to Make Your Life an Adventure

1) **Take the long view**. Time plus calamity equals comedy. So you filled the sugar bowl with salt the morning of your big dinner party. Did anybody die? No? Then, once a few weeks have passed, this is funny.

2) **Do it**. Don't sit on the sidelines and watch. Participate. So what if you look a little foolish? You're making memories.

3) **Initiate change**. Start small. Eat a new cereal for breakfast. Drive home a different route. Try a new beauty product. Life is a feast of possibilities—don't go hungry.

 ## Let the Adventures Begin!

Whether you realize it or not, your life is a great adventure. What you do, who you are and the time you live in will never be repeated. The thought of creating great family memories keeps us eager to experience life at its fullest. Scrapbookers often tell me, "Since I started scrapbooking, I go more places and participate in more activities."

This book is dedicated to the adventurous spirit in all of us.

About writing by hand...

I was admiring pages by a talented scrapbook page designer when I commented on the handwritten script. "That's gorgeous," I said.

She told me it was her handwriting and that she hated it. Well, we all hate our own handwriting, don't we? I started thinking about her distaste. I thought her handwriting looked great. Hmmm.

I decided then and there to use more of my own handwriting on my pages. We're all too critical of how we form our letters. That criticism frequently stops us from journaling. The way I see it, we can concentrate on the memories we're saving or we can moan and groan about our penmanship.

About creating pages...

This book shares simple page designs for newcomers as well as more complex page ideas for seasoned scrapbookers. As you look at the layouts, note other information we've included:

 **Supplies** are found under the picture of the traveling trunk.

 **Look Further** appears under the binoculars with valuable ready-to-use ideas illustrated by each page.

Design Tips gives suggestions for making your pages more pleasing to the eye.

 **Take Note** offers fresh thoughts about journaling in your scrapbook pages.

Adapt This Page serves up ideas for making these pages work for you.

PS accompanies pages using PostScript Paper with specific thoughts for working with this exciting new product.

Seek the adventure around you...

Every day I fall in love with the richness of the world around me. More than the words and more than the photos, I wanted to share in this book that sense of abundance and how you can tap into that sense in your life by creating pages using Paper Adventures products.

Adventures in Journaling

Keepin' it Together

SUPPLIES

Paper Adventures paper, including Parchlucent Paper in Marine, Butter Cup and Hi-Vermilion; Jill's Paper Doll World MatchMakers in Lollipop, Two-Tone Archivals in Banana Split; Classic Collection in Sugar Solid. Lettering font is *To Die For* by Lindsay Ostrom.

<u>Yoga Girls</u>—An easy layout like this is great for sharing your passions. What physical activity adds zest to your life? What friends have you made? How have you improved your well-being as a result of getting involved?

<u>Design Tip</u>: The stripes of colored Parchlucent echo the simple colors of our T-shirts. Take your color cues from colors in your photo, but don't feel you need to match the colors exactly.

<u>Adapt This Page:</u>

You can adapt this layout easily. Center a photo over four bars of colored Parchlucent, put a descriptive page title beneath the photo, and surround with torn pieces of paper sharing your random thoughts.

TAKE NOTE

What a Feeling
The journaling was handwritten, torn and then chalked around the frayed paper edge. One or two sentences comprise each block of journaling. Notice that the topics skipped around. I described who was in the photo, why I like yoga, common yoga phrases, and how yoga makes me feel.

Adventures in Journaling

 Simple Pages

Making Good Time

SUPPLIES

Paper Adventures paper, including Jill's Paper Doll World Scene-Makers in Cloudy Day; Two-Tone Archivals in Mercury and Paprika; Flannel Sheets in Sterling; Mix'n'Match Archivals Classic Collection in Licorice Solid and Sugar Solid. Lettering font by Creating Keepsakes.

TAKE NOTE

Connection Directions

Use your journaling to explain the link between photos that have no obvious connection. Share your emotions by telling your reader what surprised, delighted or impressed you.

ADAPT THIS PAGE:

1) A torn strip of paper across the top makes an effective border.

2) Outline any wording or cropped photo with a watercolor pencil to get a soft coloration.

3) Make a journaling block do double-duty as a mat behind the photo.

ROAD THRILL—Document a first-time experience. Has someone in your family become roadworthy? Were you impressed by a novice's prowess?

DESIGN TIP: A simple paper piecing of a car on a road draws your eye across the page. You can get the same effect with stickers.

LOOK FURTHER

Pencil Over

After the journaling was printed on my computer, I went over the words of the large page title "Road Thrill" with a watercolor pencil. Then I rubbed a moist cotton tip over the watercolor penciling to get the colored shading. I drew another circle of watercolor penciling around the round photo and again used a moist cotton tip to smear the color.

Adventures in Journaling

Broad Stripes, Bright Stars

SUPPLIES

Paper Adventures paper, including Jill's Paper Doll World MatchMakers in Mainland Stars, Two-Tone Archivals in Indigo and Cardinal, Parchlucent Prints in Fire Engine Red Stars, and Mix'n'Match Classic in Sugar Solid. Lettering font by Creating Keepsakes.

<u>A Sparkling Fourth</u>—How do you celebrate our nation's independence? Who do you celebrate with? How have your celebrations changed over the years?

<u>Design Tips:</u>

1) This simple page background was created by mounting five strips of Mainland Stars on a solid blue background. Because Jill's Paper Doll World MatchMakers features two patterns on one page, it's easy to get this dynamic look.

2) The mat of red stars on white is a piece of Parchlucent mounted on white paper. I turned the Parchlucent backwards (bright side down) so that the stars are seen through the transparent paper, making them slightly less vivid. That kept the stars from competing with the photo.

<u>Adapt This Page:</u>

You can cut any of the Jill's Paper Doll World MatchMakers into strips and create a background like this one with a coordinating solid paper. The MatchMakers series was designed to make great clothes for paper dolls, but can be used in many additional ways on your pages.

Tell a Story

Use your journaling to share an anecdote. Here I told how Miss Bogey (the puppy) got her name. Sure, the page is a July 4th page, but it's the perfect place to record a tidbit about Lyndsey Hohman's dog. Go beyond the obvious and take an interesting tangent.

Adventures in Journaling

A Match Made in Heaven

Paper Adventures paper, including Jill's Paper Doll World MatchMakers in Bright Blossom, Two-Tone Archivals in Aquamarine and Banana Split, and Mix'n'Match Classic Archivals in Sugar Solid. Lettering font by Creating Keepsakes.

Share Those Family Secrets

In this journaling, I shared a common trait of babies in my family—baldness! Point out long second toes, pointed eyebrows, crooked eyeteeth, dimples, slender fingers, and so on. These are not usually obvious in photos, so capture them in words.

ADAPT THIS PAGE:
Use MatchMakers for color-blocking, creating a single mat from two or more colors of paper. Plastic coated paperclips make a simple, inexpensive, colorful addition.

GRAB A SISTER AND KISS HER!—How do your family members show affection for each other? What is the relationship between siblings? How do the older children welcome new arrivals?

DESIGN TIP: Let the paper do the work for you! Creating color block pages is easy with MatchMakers. Just tape two pieces of MatchMakers together on the backside, alternating the papers, so one pattern abuts another pattern or a solid. Since each piece has two different designs (a pattern and a solid, two patterns or two solids) you can create wonderful color blocking with a minimum of effort.

Dress It Up

You don't need to repeat the pattern on people's clothes exactly, but your page will look pulled together if you repeat similar colors in your background paper.

Adventures in Journaling 9

Rough Rides, Easy Crops

Paper Adventures paper, including Mix'n'Match Archivals in Brick, Basket, Cream Solid, and Licorice Solid. Lettering font by Creating Keepsakes.

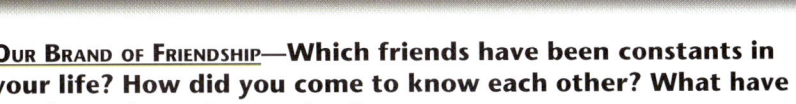

OUR BRAND OF FRIENDSHIP—Which friends have been constants in your life? How did you come to know each other? What have you been through together?

DESIGN TIP: I didn't like the cluttered background behind us, so I created a new one. First I cropped the photo to expose only the two of us and the booth, then I added another photo behind us for the background. The key to creative cropping is to find natural lines along which to crop the photo like the edge of the wood paneling around our restaurant booth.

ADAPT THIS PAGE:

You could re-use this layout for any visit to a restaurant or special place. Get in the habit of taking photos of signage and fascias and storefronts. Instead of a sign, you could include a copy of a menu or program.

It All Started When…

Tell the history of your friendship. This journaling covers 17 years of friendship in brief. When you have a lot to write in a small amount of space, use computer lettering. Most of us can write smaller on computer than by hand.

Adventures in Journaling

Take a Solid Swing

SUPPLIES

Paper Adventures paper, including Mix'n'Match Classic in Sugar Solid, Licorice Solid and Lime Solid; and k.p. kids & co. in Field of Greens. Lettering font by Creating Keepsakes.

Dreams of Green

Show how your dreams have grown and changed. This journaling tells how Peter has met one of his life goals and how his continuing love of golf is shared now with his sons. Notice that Peter in the large photo with Jack Nicklaus is about the same age as his son James in the small photo. If you restrict yourself to scrapping chronologically, you'll miss chances to make comparisons like this.

SUITS US TO A T—What youthful dreams of yours have come true? Who have you idolized along the way? How have you passed your interests on to your children?

DESIGN TIP: Notice how the black background picks up the black in the pattern of the Field of Greens grass. Don't be afraid to use black as a background to your pages.

ADAPT THIS PAGE:

A strip of color like the green here makes an effective mat for one or more photos. Or, you could recycle this layout and put the journaling box where the second small photo is. No scratch golfers in the family? Why not visit a put-put golf center?

Adventures in Journaling

Leafing the Country

SUPPLIES

Paper Adventures paper, including Velveteen Paper in Sage, Hot Potatoes Quadrants in Not Just Greens, Two-Tone Archivals in Paprika, and Jill's Paper Doll World MatchMakers for Skin in Tan and MatchMakers for Clothes in City Plaid. Leaf punch is a Paper Adventures Punch Wheel (Leaves). Lettering template by Scrap Pagerz.

TAKE NOTE

Professional Tour Guides

You personally don't have to write every word that appears in your pages. I could not have improved upon this wonderful quotation from Bill Bryson. If you are interested in England, I recommend his book *Notes from a Small Island*.

COUNTRY WALKS—What restores your soul? How do you get back to nature? Where is your favorite spot to commune with the flora and the fauna?

DESIGN TIP: The leaves near the journaling box were punched out first, then arranged as desired. Finally, I pressed a thin strip of paper with adhesive on the back onto the leaves. The strip holds the leaves in place.

ADAPT THIS PAGE:
Try a meandering piece of paper behind your photos to tie your page design together. A somber meandering piece will tone down a bright background, and a bright meandering piece will add color interest.

Adventures in Journaling

Moods of Paper

Foot-Tapping Textures

SUPPLIES

Paper Adventures paper, including Velveteen Paper in Wedgwood, Two-Tone Archivals in Green Tea, and Mix'n'Match Classic Archivals in Sugar Solid and Licorice Solid. Lettering font by Creating Keepsakes.

TAKE NOTE

Peanut Butter Rocks

Give your readers details. Minutia makes it real. I wrote that Presley's serves one of Elvis' favorite foods, fried peanut butter and banana sandwiches. A small tidbit, but one that evokes visions of Elvis.

ADAPT THIS PAGE:
You could change the color on these shoes and tell a story about how fast kids' feet grow or how your husband always wears wingtips. Or reproduce the "Blue Suede Shoes" and tell your own Elvis story.

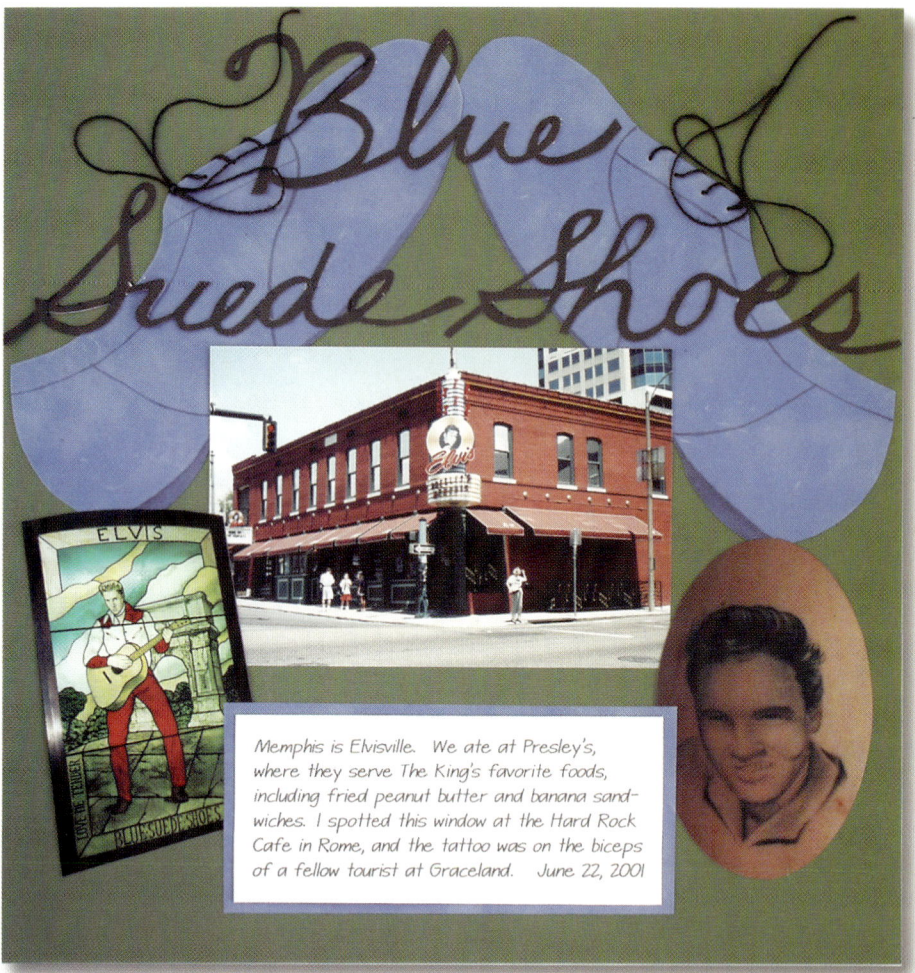

Memphis is Elvisville. We ate at Presley's, where they serve The King's favorite foods, including fried peanut butter and banana sandwiches. I spotted this window at the Hard Rock Cafe in Rome, and the tattoo was on the biceps of a fellow tourist at Graceland.   June 22, 2001

BLUE SUEDE SHOES—Which musicians do you enjoy? Where are their musical roots? How do you and other fans celebrate their musical careers?

DESIGN TIP: To create the page title, I wrote the words "Blue Suede Shoes" in crayon. I went back and thickened the lettering to the size I wanted. I adhered the words to the Licorice Solid with a temporary adhesive. Using a piece of glass beneath my paper, I first cut out the center of the letters with a craft knife and then I cut out the rest of the word.

LOOK FURTHER

More Than Skin Deep
Yes, that's actually a photo of a tattoo of Elvis on a man's arm. We were standing side by side in the line to see Graceland. I debated, but in the end the scrapbooker in me couldn't resist such a funky photo. (I asked permission first, just in case.)

Adventures in Journaling

Moods of Paper

Mouth-Watering Velveteen

SUPPLIES

Paper Adventures paper, including Velveteen Paper in Cranberry, Two-Tone Archivals in Bubble Gum, Jill's Paper Doll World MatchMakers in Sunday Best, Hot Potatoes Quadrants in Curly Whirl, Parchlucent Paper in Peony, and Mulberry Paper in Sugar. Lettering font by Creating Keepsakes.

PERSIAN NIGHTS—**Who has introduced you to foods from different cultures? What cultures have you learned about? What did you eat?**

DESIGN TIPS:

1) To tear Mulberry Paper, fold it along the desired line, lick the fold and pull gently apart. I wanted the top and bottom edges on my journaling to look very soft, so I pulled apart Mulberry Paper twice and used two layers of frayed edges.

2) These beautiful gold-headed straight pins came from the sewing department of a big department store. Look for special "additions" in stationery and craft stores— look also in hardware stores, sewing departments, kid's toy departments and gift shops.

Crisp Printing

The journaling is printed directly on the Parchlucent Paper. Because Parchlucent is crisp, your ink won't run or smear. Ordinary vellums often absorb too much ink and make your printing look fuzzy. If you like the look of ink on transparent paper, you'll love Parchlucent Paper.

The Head-Hand Connection

The day after our Persian feast I made a list of all the foods Camilla had prepared. Later I lost the list, but because I had written it down, I could remember the dishes. A look at the photo confirmed my powers of recall. Train yourself to write down information. With or without the list in hand, you'll have a better memory to draw on.

Adventures in Journaling

Moods of Paper

The Color of Love

SUPPLIES

Paper Adventures paper, including Jill's Paper Doll World SceneMakers in Winter Plaid; Velveteen Paper in Ruby; k.p. kids & co. in Flower Showers; Two-Tone Archivals in Petunia, Brown Sugar and Green Tea. Lettering font by Creating Keepsakes.

TAKE NOTE

Love Songs

Your scrapbook is a great place to record your love for your family. Think about the people you love. Have you written about that love in your scrapbook?

ADAPT THIS PAGE:

Run a simple banner page title across your page top and hang shapes from it. Adjust the lengths of the shapes to emphasize your photographed subjects. Also note the journaling block on the right that balances the page title on the left.

TRUE LOVE WAYS—How do you share your love for family? Who do you appreciate? Where do they live and how do you feel about their home?

DESIGN TIP: Note the date above the portrait. By shifting the photo low on the mat, the date itself is matted. Mats don't have to be even on all sides. In fact, you'll have more options if you cut your mats large so you can play with the widths. Trim them down after you've discovered your best option.

LOOK FURTHER

Ruby Red Repeating

The deep ruby velvet curtains behind Margaret and Mike are repeated with the warm Velveteen Paper. Notice that the front door of the house is the same color. A lucky coincidence.

Adventures in Journaling 15

Facing Pages, Facing Photos

Paper Adventures paper, including PostScript Papers in Blueberry Plaid, Two-Tone Archivals in Indigo and Banana Split, and Mix'n'Match Classic Archivals in Sugar Solid. Self-Stick Lettering by Paper Adventures in Daffodil and Blueberry. Lettering font by Creating Keepsakes.

<u>Do you bleed</u> **BLUE?**—You do if you live in St. Louis. What sports do you follow? Which sports heroes attract your attention? Where do you go to see your favorite teams perform?

<u>Design Tips:</u>

1) Notice how each photo faces inward. Our eyes naturally follow the line of sight of others' eyes. This keeps the focus on the center of the page.

2) To place letter stickers, line up the bottom edges on a ruler. Press the top of letters onto the paper, then roll the ruler away from the letter bottoms.

<u>Adapt This Page:</u>

Use a large element as a backdrop for your photos. The large element ties your page together. The more simple and striking the element is, the better this works.

Be a Ticket Taker
The Blues logo was copied and enlarged from a ticket, and then pieced together. Hang on to tickets and memorabilia for use in creating page elements. You never know what you will need and if you don't have it, you can't use it.

Background Information

Use your journaling as a place to explain "how this came to be." How did you come to be fans of this team? How did you wind up with tickets? Events don't usually happen in a vacuum, so write about the circumstances behind your photos.

16　　　　　　　　　　　　　　　　　　　　**Adventures in Journaling**

 *PostScript Paper*

A Full Count with Photos

SUPPLIES

Paper Adventures paper, including PostScript Paper in Fire Engine Red Stripe, Parchlucent Paper in Crystal, and Mix'n'Match Archivals Classic Collection in Ruby Solid and Sugar Solid. Lettering font by Creating Keepsakes.

TAKE NOTE

Details from the Dugout

Write about what can't be seen in your photos. Concentrate on the emotions and the action.

LOOK FURTHER

It's in the Cards

The "close-up" of Mark McGwire is actually a promotional card. You can encapsulate such an item in an archivally safe page protector cut to size, as I did, or scan the item and reproduce it.

CARDINALS—Here we are cheering our home team. Who do you go to games with? What have you learned from them about your favorite sport? What do you enjoy doing together at the games?

PS:

I positioned extra photos along a strip of red paper at the top of the page to tell the story of Mark McGwire breaking Roger Maris' record. Then I explained the photos in my journaling. Small pictures like these are perfect to use under your Page Flipper. Along with the journaling, they sequentially tell a powerful story.

DESIGN TIPS:

1) The page title came from an advertisement in the *St. Louis Post Dispatch*. I copied the title on my light box. When you travel, pick up a local newspaper for useful designs like this.

2) Watch what others do. Julie is a better sports photographer than I'll ever be, so I pay attention. When she takes a picture, so do I.

Adventures in Journaling 17

A Parade of Possibilities

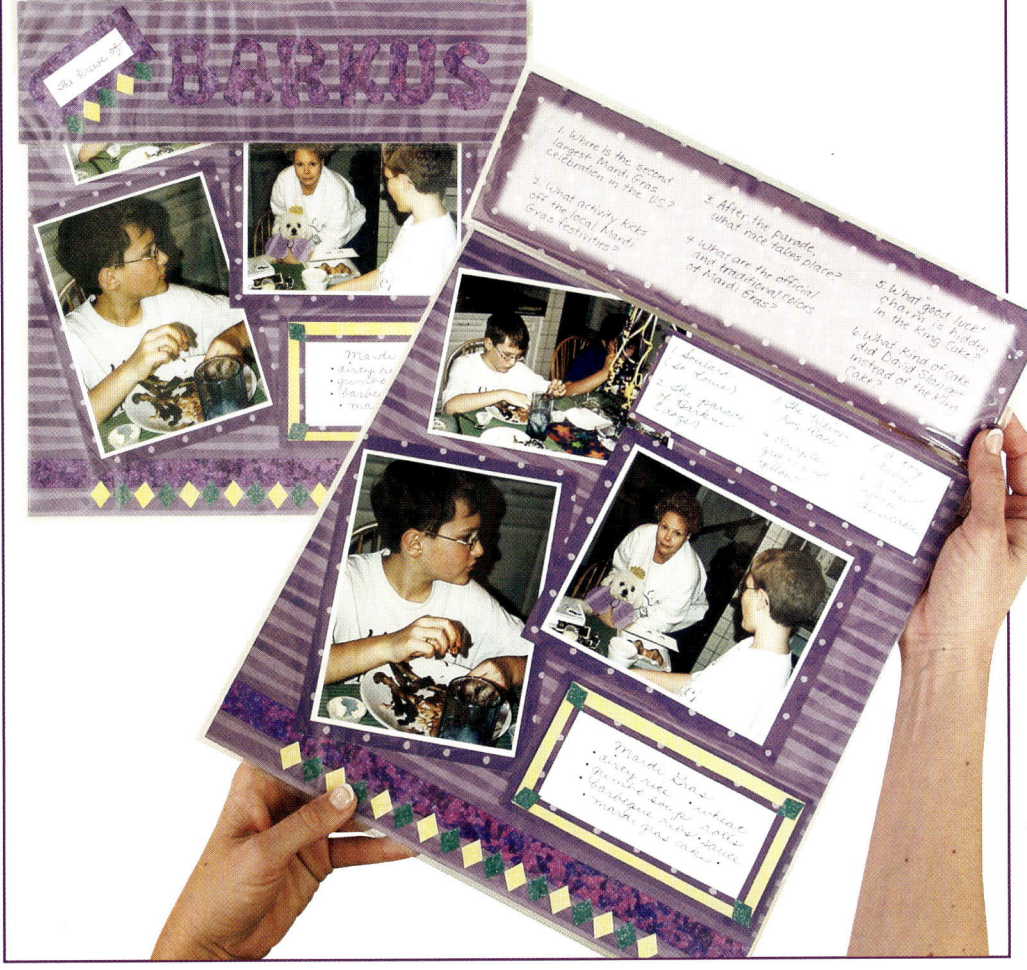

THE KREWE OF BARKUS—Party hardy. What local festivities do you celebrate at home? What's on the menu? What is the history of this event?

DESIGN TIP—The page title letters were traced from the template onto the journaling strip of the PostScript Paper. Then I carefully cut out each letter with a craft knife. I backed the letters with ribbon, taping the ribbon securely on the reverse side. I backed the first page title with another journaling strip, sandwiching the taped side between the two journaling strips.

Bowed Over
Ever have a problem like this? The bow our dog was wearing was red. It clashed with the rest of the page. I put tissue paper over the bow and traced it. Then I cut a bow out of the PostScript Paper and glued it onto the photo.

Paper Adventures paper, including PostScript Papers in Grape Stripe and Dots, Diamond Dust in Evergreen, Sunflower and Grape, and Mix'n'Match Archivals Classic Collection in Sugar Solid. Lettering template by Scrap Pagerz.

Background Information
I included our menu and a nifty quiz I created about Mardi Gras traditions. I found a wealth of information about Mardi Gras on the web. The quiz questions appear on the inside of the Page Flipper and the answers appear underneath on the main page. Since the quiz isn't visually exciting, the Page Flipper gave me a tidy way to save what I learned.

Adventures in Journaling

Seeing Double-Stuff

SUPPLIES

Paper Adventures paper, including PostScript Papers in Sunflower Dots; Jill's Paper Doll World SceneMakers in Nature Green and Cement; Mix'n'Match Archivals Classic Collection in Grape Polkadots, Licorice Solid and Sugar Solid; and Parchlucent Paper in Crystal. Stickers by Mrs. Grossman's.

TAKE NOTE

Loving That Oreo

My journaling here serves to mark a special occasion: a new addition to the Singer family. Besides the simple "who, what, when, where and why," I added an observation that Oreo's feet probably never touched the ground her first days at home.

KATIE'S NEW PUP OREO—Who's new in your neighborhood? How have your neighborhood children grown? What pets are familiar sights on your block? (I admit, I know some people by their dogs.)

DESIGN TIPS:

1) Getting Katie and Oreo to hold still was impossible, so I combined two photos (one of Katie and one of Oreo) and added a leash to tie the two together. Silhouette crop your subjects first, and then play with the visual elements for inspiration.

2) Cutting rings as I did here with the black paper is easier if you cut out the center first and then the outside edge.

ADAPT THIS PAGE:

You could use these cookies as portholes if you are doing a cruise page or you could do an Oreo page. Show how much fun it is to eat the middle first.

PS:

Think of your PostScript journaling strip as a door with windows onto your background page, as I've done here.

Adventures in Journaling

Find Your Thrill

SUPPLIES

Paper Adventures paper, including PostScript Papers in Blueberry Plaid and Blueberry Flowers, Two-Tone Archivals in Bubble Gum, Jill's Paper Doll World Match-Makers in Posy Garden, and Mix 'n' Match Archivals Classic Collection in Sugar and Blueberry Solid.

<u>Mile High Pie</u>—My, oh my! What caused you to take a detour on the way home? What local delicacy was irresistible? What did you bring home to share?

<u>Design Tips:</u>

1) Since the PostScript Papers work together, I used two patterns to make this page feel "homey." Then I used solid Blueberry along with the pink to color block one photo and to mat the pie.

2) The tile letter "e" juts out slightly from the Page Flipper. A slit in the Page Flipper allowed me to attach the word "PIE" by slipping it in from the side (I'd already put adhesive on the back).

TAKE NOTE

Photo Journalism

As I explained in my journaling, the reason we stopped was to buy a pie for my husband's birthday. Well, that's our story and we're sticking to it. By including the signage (both outside the restaurant and inside), I included all sorts of details that I was then able to leave out of my journaling.

LOOK FURTHER

Penning a Faux Mat
The lettering tiles are matted with pens twice before being truly matted on Bubble Gum (a vibrant pink paper). The pink "mat" is a broken pen line and the blue "mat" is a solid edge.

<u>PS:</u>

Note that in addition to the patterns, PostScript Paper gives you a solid on the reverse side.

Great Ideas for Journaling with PostScript Paper

Paper Adventures paper, including Jill's Paper Doll World MatchMakers in Geranium Weave, PostScript Papers in Blueberry Plaid and Stripe, Parchlucent Prints in Grass Green and Fire Engine Red Polkadots, Diamond Dust in (red and green), Flannel Sheet in Sugar, and Mix 'n'Match Archivals Classic Collection in Sugar Solid. Self-Stick Lettering by Paper Adventures in Ruby and Green.

1. **Give it a title**. A page with a page title will demand your reader's attention. The person looking at the page uses the title to understand what's happening—quickly! Decide where your page title will go in relation to the PS 3" x 12" detachable strip.

2. **Line it up**. The lightly lined back of the PS journaling band is perfect for hand lettering. Plus, you can also journal on the part of the page directly beneath the PS journaling band by adding a solid-colored journaling box. Yes, you can double your journaling space and not give up even an inch of your 12" x 12" page!

3. **Which end is up?** Consider which end will be up when someone opens your journaling band. You don't want to wind up with upside down sentiments.

4. **A perfect match**. Paper Adventures makes lettering stickers in colors that match the PS Paper perfectly. Since the colors of the PS Paper all work together, you can mix and match lettering stickers with gusto.

5. **Surprise, surprise!** I like to use the PS as a sort of "surprise" in my storytelling. Because people won't see the hidden area until last, you can put the "shocking" ending underneath for a cool ta-dah type reaction.

6. **Safe for small photos**. On the area covered by the PS Paper, I've been having fun putting small cropped photos that wouldn't make it on the page otherwise. We're talking photos that were small, needed cropping or just weren't your best.

7. **Include a P.S.** Direct mail professionals swear that the P.S. (from "postscriptum" which is Latin for *later writing*) is the best read part of any letter. Think of this as a high impact area for sharing your thoughts.

GRANDPA CLAUS—**How have the children in your family reacted to visits with Santa? With joy or trepidation? Notice that Paddy is not comfortable with his Grandfather's disguise.**

Adventures in Journaling

Bounce & Flip It

SUPPLIES

Paper Adventures paper, including Jill's Paper Doll World MatchMakers in Posy Garden, Bud and Plaid, Two-Tone Archivals in Bubble Gum, Mix'n'Match Archivals Heirloom Collection in Sage Speckle and Sugar Solid. Edging and template from Puzzle-Mates. Lettering template by Scrap Pagerz.

TAKE NOTE

I Remember When...

Has a recent situation reminded you of your youth? Record the link between then and now. You may not have a photo of yourself bouncing on the bed, but you can re-create your memory with a photo of other children.

<u>BOUNCING ON THE BED</u>—**Where have you been a house guest? What did you enjoy about your host's household? Who else was a guest with you?**

<u>DESIGN TIPS</u>:

1) The white stripe that travels across the page and over the oval photo helps to bring out the white in the photos and to direct your eye.

2) To create a 12" stretch of Posy Garden, I joined two pieces of paper and hid the seam under the pink stripe. (Note: this paper is now available in 12" x 12".)

<u>PS</u>:

The area under your Page Flipper can be a separate but related story. Here I showed photos of Daniele at the neighborhood pool, the Todorov's home, and their cat.

Scan and Reduce

The photos on the reverse side of the Page Flipper were scanned and reduced slightly to fit the space. Scanning and reducing is a wonderful alternative to cropping.

<u>ADAPT THIS PAGE</u>:

You can reproduce this layout with a Puzzle-Mate template or create your own modification of the template.

22 *Adventures in Journaling*

A Storybook Wedding

SUPPLIES

Paper Adventures paper, including Parchlucent Paper in Gold Nugget and Crystal/Opal, Two-Tone Archivals in Green Tea, and Mix'n'Match Archivals Classic Collection in Sugar Solid.

LOOK FURTHER

Decorate It!
The photo of Jenni's bouquet makes a stunning addition to the page and echoes the flowers in the border. Be sure to take photos of accoutrements like flowers, rings, cakes, pew decorations, table favors and so on to add to your wedding pages.

ADAPT THIS PAGE:
You could put a floral border like this around any set of photos. The template is large enough that your pen ball fits into the openings perfectly, making tracing easy to do.

LANCE AND JENNI—Whose romance have you seen blossom? What do you enjoy about attending weddings? Why were you invited to participate?

DESIGN TIP: Figure out where the border will begin and end before you start to ink in the design. Modify the length of the border by adding flowers or putting different streamers together. As you can see, the light ink on the dark paper looks wonderful. A hint of chalk around parts of the border helped soften the look. I also added dots, the ubiquitous and indispensable design aid.

PS:
The Page Flipper holds the page title "Lance and Jenni" and provides a space underneath for my journaling and a photo of the couple. Remember that when you open up the Page Flipper, your writing must read from top to bottom. Do a test before you glue down your pieces.

Adventures in Journaling

Page Flippers

Egging On a Greeting

SUPPLIES

Paper Adventures paper, including Jill's Paper Doll World SceneMakers in Spring Plaid; Parchlucent Prints in Rose Polkadots and Grape Polkadots; Two-Tone Archivals in Blue Jay, Wild Berry and African Violet; and Mix'n'Match Archivals Classic Collection in Sugar Solid. Self-Stick Lettering by Paper Adventures in Rose. Snowflake punch by Paper Adventures Punch Wheel (Christmas) and heart punch by Paper Adventures Punch Wheel (Classic).

<u>Getting the Color Eggxactly Right</u>—It's fun to dye for. What are your spring time traditions? How do you prepare for them? Who participates?

<u>Design Tips</u>:

1) The phrase "getting the color" is handwritten on white and matted, the short phrase is combined with the fancy words "eggxactly right." Try this combination headline technique whenever you have a lead-in phrase and a few words you want to spotlight.

2) To get the stripes of color on the word "egg" I first created the striped paper and then cut out the letters.

<u>Adapt This Page</u>:

This mosaic look would work well on any subject. In particular, I think it lends itself to an artsy type of activity. Also different solid papers under your Parchlucent will give you different textures and colors. Take a little time and experiment.

Space to Fill

This page has a bit of a mosaic look with "empty" space filled by a punch art strip or a strip of Polkadot Parchlucent Prints backed with white paper. Lay out your photos and journaling boxes first, then fill in around them.

<u>PS:</u>

I added a seasonal greeting. When the Page Flipper is open, the greeting adds a cheery note.

Adventures in Journaling

A Place for All Senses

SUPPLIES

Paper Adventures paper, including Parchlucent Paper in Moonlight, Citron and Wine; Two-Tone Archivals in Root Beer, Peaches 'n' Cream, and Grasshopper, Flannel Sheets in Licorice, PostScript Papers in Sunflower Plaid, and Mix'n'Match Archivals Classic Collection in Sugar Solid. "Egg" lettering template by Scrap Pagerz. Wave Mammoth Edge Accents decorative scissors by Paper Adventures.

GROSSOLOGY!—Ooops. What didn't turn out the way you planned? Why not? What happened as a result?

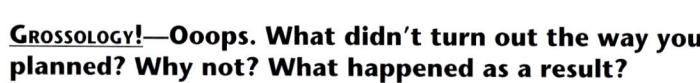

DESIGN TIP: Running your headline across several pages ties the lay-outs together. Use a re-positional adhesive and you can move the letters around until you like what you see.

TAKE NOTE

Getting the Muck for Yuck

I made notes at the exhibit and I took photos of signage. The notes and signage gave me the gross but accurate copy that appears in the splats under "Oh, yuck." I also journaled the boys' reaction to an entire exhibit of body functions.

LOOK FURTHER

Pig Tales

The garbage pile with the pig on top was recreated using a photo of the pig to form the right hand border of the pages.

PS:

The "who, what, when, where, why and how" are handwritten in narrative form on the reverse side of the PostScript Paper. The guidelines for your writing are already printed on the PostScript Paper.

Adventures in Journaling   25

Page Flippers

Color in Harmony with Paper

LAND IN HARMONY WITH NATURE—How have the people around you carved out their own little pieces of heaven? What do you admire about your friends or neighbors?

DESIGN TIP: While this page looks complicated, it's just a central portrait framed by photos and writing that open. Once the photo of Michael was in place, I measured out where the Page Flippers would fall around the portrait. Then I placed the photos and journaling on the background page within those parameters.

SUPPLIES

Paper Adventures paper, including Two-Tone Archivals in Emerald, Jasper and Pewter, Mix'n'Match Archivals Collection in Sugar Solid. Lettering font by Creating Keepsakes.

TAKE NOTE

Using Quotations
While I was contemplating this page, I came across the quotation by the American naturalist John Burroughs. Keep track of quotations and thoughts that speak to you for future use on pages.

LOOK FURTHER

Shabby Chic
I fatigued the paper by sanding it—this is the "Shabby Chic" technique taught to me by Angie Randall of PaperKuts Magazine. This technique only works with papers that have a white core such as those from Paper Adventures. This technique is also shown on page 26.

ADAPT THIS PAGE:
Adapt this page design by centering a portrait or quotation in the middle of a 12" x 12" page and creating a frame of Page Flippers.

PS:
Plan for your page with the Page Flippers open and closed.

26 Adventures in Journaling

Page Flippers

Jumping Up Geraniums

SUPPLIES

Paper Adventures paper, including Parchlucent Prints in Grass Green Polkadots; Parchlucent Paper in Crystal, Honey, Peony and Moss; Two-Tone Archivals in Green Tea and Bubble Gum; and Mix'n'Match Archivals Collection in Sugar Solid.

TAKE NOTE

Save What Matters Most

Rarely do we take the time to write about what matters. It mattered to me that my house had flowers. It mattered to me that the woman moving in would be able to enjoy their pink blossoms. Make a list of what matters to you and commit it to a scrapbook page.

ADAPT THIS PAGE:
Add memorabilia that goes beyond pieces of paper to your pages. Lightweight plastic is easy to adhere.

IN THE PINK—What don't you want to forget? What current activities bring meaning to your life? What activities are tied to where you live?

DESIGN TIPS:

1) To create the transparent flower pot, I punched flowers and leaves, cut out the pot, assembled all the pieces and adhered the pieces to a clear overhead projector transparency. Then I covered the transparency with archival film. The finished pot was slipped into a Page Flipper.

2) I printed the page title, then I traced it with my light box so the letters overlapped.

LOOK FURTHER

Go on a Stake Out
The information stakes that came with the plants enhance my page. Memorabilia like this makes your pages more "real."

PS:
Use Parchlucent Paper to make a design that covers journaling. How about creating a sun, a rainbow or a cloud? I love the way this journaling peeps around the Parchlucent flowerpot.

Adventures in Journaling

 **Page Flippers**

Step-by-Step Storytelling

WHERE IS MIKE'S FROG?—What unexpected "dramas" does your family still laugh about today? What happened? How was it resolved?

> **DESIGN TIP:** Before you glue anything down, lay out all your pieces to see that your flaps fit over your photos. Trim your photos a tiny bit at a time. Add numbers to your flaps to make the sequence more clear.

PS: You can turn the Page Flipper so that it adheres on any side because the adhesive strip is crystal clear. You can also reposition it.

SUPPLIES

Paper Adventures paper, including PostScript Papers in Grass Green Plaid and Mix'n'Match Archivals Collection in Sugar Solid.

ADAPT THIS PAGE:

Look through children's peek-a-boo books to get ideas for similar pages. What do you search for in your house? What do you do step by step? Either would make a good lift-the-flap page—and, with Page-Flippers, kids can handle the pages again and again without worry of photos being damaged by acidic hands.

TAKE NOTE

And Then What Happened? Consider family stories you might want to tell in sequence. Think: What happened first? Second? Third? And the end result? Let these questions guide you as you write.

LOOK FURTHER

A Hopping Die Cut A plain die cut of a frog was transformed with a little ink and chalk. It helps to have a picture of the real item (the frog) in front of you as you work on shading your die cut. Remember you can erase chalk. I like to shape my chalked shading by erasing away layers of color because the eraser seems to give me more control than the applicator.

Star-Spangled Apple

Sparkling Pages

SUPPLIES

Paper Adventures paper, including Two-Tone Archivals in Indigo, Grasshopper and Brown Sugar; Mix'n'Match Archivals Classic Collection in Sugar Solid; Mulberry Paper in Sugar; and Diamond Dust in Ruby. Self-Stick Lettering by Paper Adventures in Ruby and Sugar. Lettering font by Creating Keepsakes.

TAKE NOTE

Ask the Right Questions

I interviewed Lesley and made notes about the visit. I said, "Tell me how you happened to photograph this policeman." The words "tell me how" open the door to a full explanation. Avoid asking "yes" or "no" questions.

ADAPT THIS PAGE:
You could use a similar page title and apple shape to discuss a favorite teacher or an apple pie.

TAKING A SHINE TO THE BIG APPLE—The spirit of New Yorkers, their warmth and gratitude, shines in this layout. When Lesley Hindmarsh and Carolyn Conner showed me their photos, I had to make a page honoring the indomitable spirit that the United Kingdom and the United States have in common.

DESIGN TIP: Overlapping visual elements lead your eye around a page. By putting the apple over the journaling, your eyes are drawn into the text.

LOOK FURTHER

Repeating Stars & Stripes
The flying American flags lining the street to the Empire State Building repeat the image of the flag hanging behind Laura, James and the police officer. The flag's colors are repeated on the page, but the sense of the flying flags is repeated also in the strips of Mulberry Paper that wave from behind the photos.

Adventures in Journaling

Jumping Into Sparkling Water

Paper Adventures paper, including k.p. kids & co. in Blue Swirls and Twirls, Two-Tone Archivals in Blueberry, Mix'n'-Match Archivals Classic Collection in Sugar Solid, and Diamond Dust in Blueberry.

Characteristic Photos

When Elaine first shared these photos, she told me about Daniele's confidence. I added my own observations about Daniele's character to the anecdote of her first deep-end jump. Use your journaling to explain your images.

SPLASH—**Think of the first time you or a member of your family tried something. Looking back, did you put off trying out of fear? Did conquering fear once give you confidence to try something else that was new?**

DESIGN TIPS:

1) An oval cutter was used to round the sides of the top photo. Use the oval cutter first (when your photo is largest), and then trim the top and bottom of the image.
2) Trimming the Blue Swirls and Twirls to represent rippling water adds a sense of action to the page.

ADAPT THIS PAGE:

You could put any water photos on a similar background. Remember the rule of thirds. Break your page into thirds and cover at least 2/3 with either a solid or the print for visual harmony.

Deep-Sea Shooting

One photo was taken with an underwater camera. Elaine positioned herself where her daughter would go under. After several tries, Elaine was able to snap this perfect picture.

30 Adventures in Journaling

Glamour in Glitter

SUPPLIES

Paper Adventures paper, including Parchlucent Paper in Gold Nugget and Crystal/Metallic, Mix'n'Match Archivals Classic Collection in Licorice Solid and Sugar Solid, Two-Tone Archivals in Licorice, Velveteen Paper in Licorice and Diamond Dust in Licorice. Lettering fonts by Creating Keepsakes.

Information Online

I found information on Losely Park at www.aboutbritain.com/LoselyPark.htm. I rewrote the information for my journaling. The more information you have the easier it is to write. Take the time to gather your information and then do your journaling. You'll be surprised at how much more smoothly your writing will go.

ENCHANTED EVENING—What charity events have you attended? What dressy functions have you and your mate "gussied up" for? What were your surroundings like?

DESIGN TIP: Black paper appears in three textures on this page: Diamond Dust, Velveteen and Two-Tone Paper. Instead of introducing more colors, add more textures to your page. The additional textures work especially well when you have a formal layout.

Bauble It!
The gold washers came in a pack with paper fasteners from Ryman. Pick up trinkets like these when you see them. If you have them, you'll find a way to work them into your pages.

ADAPT THIS PAGE:

The piece of Parchlucent in Crystal/Metallic running down the center of the page pulls all the pieces together. You could create a similar page using any patterned paper in the center of a 12" x 12" piece of solid paper.

Adventures in Journaling

Cap It Off With Journaling

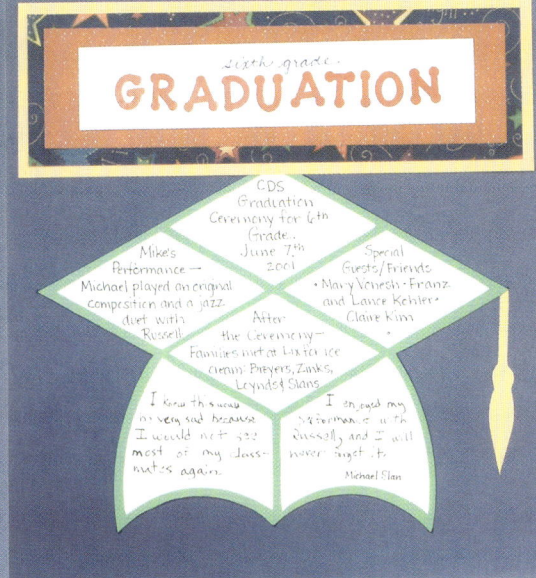

SIXTH GRADE GRADUATION—How have your children exceeded your expectations? What moments brought tears to your eyes? How did others react?

DESIGN TIP: Six layers of mat surround this posed photo. Vary the width of your mats. I also like to alternate from solid to pattern. Speckles, like the brick paper here, are a safe pattern for those of us who are a bit timid when it comes to mixing patterns up.

ADAPT THIS PAGE:

1) Use a page template to lay out your journaling. Simply put the journaling where the photos would normally go.

2) Face a posed photo with a page of journaling. Don't try to squeeze your journaling in under the picture, but give both the photo and the story the space they deserve.

Tales of Tassels
Instead of using the graduation cap page template for cutting photos, I used it to create journaling blocks. Start by cutting out the inside parts of the template and then move to the outside edges.

SUPPLIES

Paper by Paper Adventures, including k.p. kids & co. in Star Bright, Two-Tone Archivals in Grasshopper and Marigold, Mix'n'Match Archivals Classic Collection in Navy Solid and Sugar Solid, and Mix'n'Match Archivals Heirloom Collection in Brick Speckle. Self-Stick Lettering by Paper Adventures in Brick. Deckle Edge Accents scissors by Paper Adventures.

More Than One Voice
You don't have to do all the journaling yourself. I asked Michael to write a few of his thoughts about graduation night. (Yes, I bribed him, but good help is hard to find.) Now I have his viewpoint in his handwriting.

32   Adventures in Journaling

 **Whimsical Travels & Destinations**

Paper Adventures paper, including k.p. kids & co. in Wave Whimsy, Two-Tone Archivals in Grape, Mix'n'Match Archivals Classic Collection in Sugar and Wedgwood Solid. Self-Stick Lettering by Paper Adventures in Grape.

Over the River and Through the Woods

This journaling evolved from a handwritten scrap of paper with directions on it. What directions have you saved? Ever had directions that led you astray? Share the directions and tell us the rest of your story in your journaling.

ADAPT THIS PAGE:
Hang on to directions for getting places or doing things and tell what happened. Did you make that recipe but leave out the baking powder? Commit your faux pas to a page.

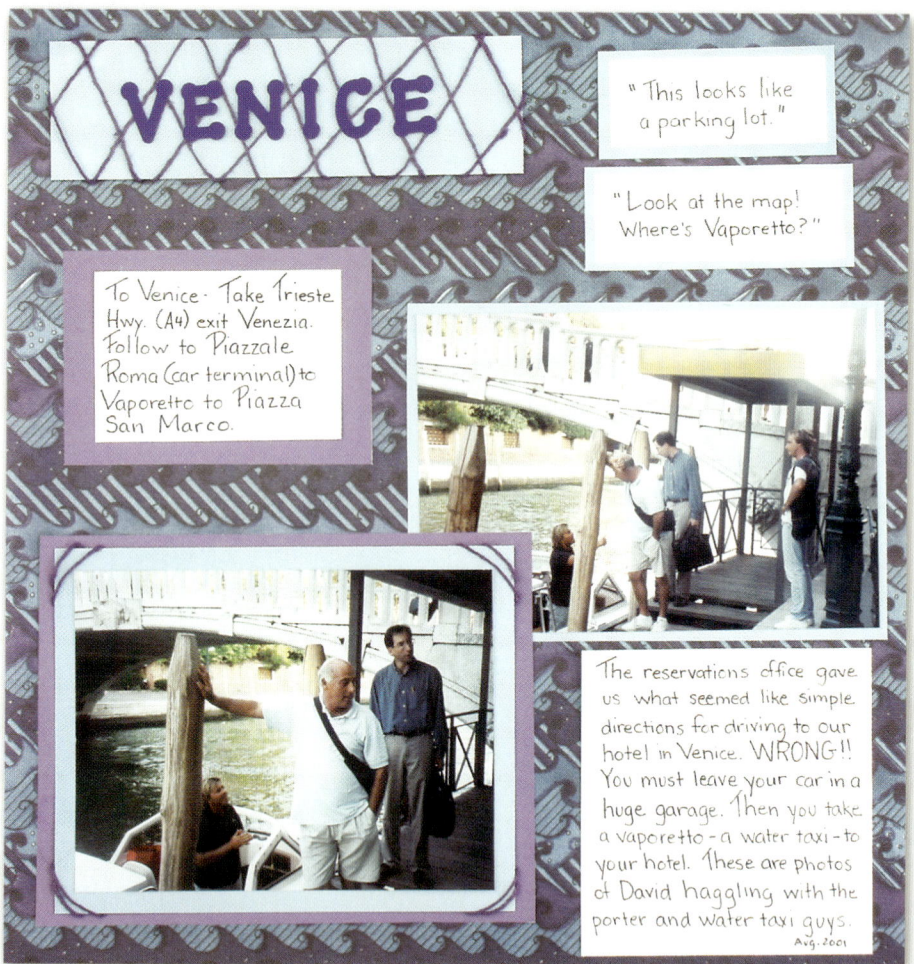

VENICE—What directions have baffled you? What did you do or say when you discovered you were lost? What do you know now that you didn't know then?

DESIGN TIPS:
1) Use hemp as a pattern under your lettering. Wrap the hemp around a paper strip and tape the hemp on the back to keep it from slipping.

2) Wrap a bit of hemp over a mat corner for added texture. Tape it on the backside.

So Clear it's Transparent
The crisscross design on the guardrail around the canal inspired me to crisscross hemp over a piece of blue paper. The self-stick lettering was applied to a piece of overhead transparency and then tucked behind the laced hemp. You can use this simple page title over and over again with different colors of lettering, hemp and background paper.

Adventures in Journaling

The Spirit of Scrapbooking

SPIRIT OF ST. LOUIS—What school events has your child participated in? What impressions loomed large after the event? Who did your child pal around with during the event?

DESIGN TIP: I twisted the blue wire into a loop, then I tacked the loop down on each corner with a "stitch" of taupe wire. The wire is subtle, but it adds interest and dimension to the journaling block.

SUPPLIES

Paper Adventures paper, including Jill's Paper Doll World SceneMakers in Earth Plaid; Mix'n'Match Archivals Collection in Slate Solid and Sage Speckle, and Sugar Solid; Velveteen Paper in Sage; and Hot Potatoes Quadrants in Not Just Greens. Lettering template by Scrap Pagerz.

ADAPT THIS PAGE:

1) Try a little twisted wire where you might put a photo corner. Tape the wire behind your paper to keep the wire secure.

2) Running a border down the outside edges of your pages organizes your visual elements. Since the Not Just Greens paper is only 11" long, I had to cheat. I stopped the border under the photos and started it up again coming out of the photos.

Write Around the Clock

Beginning counter-clockwise, I journaled by describing each photo and its subjects in turn. Allow your photos to prompt your writing when the pictures are rich like these are.

Working Together

To get continuity across two pages, I taped the pages together on the reverse side and worked with them as though they were one big page. You can see how this gives tremendous freedom in designing a really big story.

34 Adventures in Journaling

You Can Pick These Daisies

Paper Adventures paper, including PostScript Paper in Sunflower Flowers and Plaid, Velveteen Paper in Daffodil, Quadrants Papercrafting Packs in Grass Green Classic, and Mix'n'Match Archivals Classic Collection in Sugar Solid and Grass Green Solid. Mammoth Edge Accents scissors in Ruffle by Paper Adventures. Appliqué by Wrights.

CRAZY DAISY—What member of your family keeps you laughing out loud? How would you describe this person? What do they do?

DESIGN TIPS:

1) Think odd. Scatter your embellishments around your layout in odd numbers. Otherwise we tend to pair things up and that's boring.

2) The big daisies have Flannel Paper centers. So plush.

3) To make the big daisies, I drew big circles, then cut the circles out with scalloped decorative scissors. Once I had the scallops, I cut toward the center of the circle to create the petals.

ADAPT THIS PAGE:

1) If you only have one small photo play it up by putting it smack dab in the center of your page and ring it with your page title.

2) Make your journaling interactive. As you pull down the journaling strip, you can read paragraph after paragraph but the photo remains the center of attraction.

Behind the Scene

Behind the page is a sleeve slightly larger than the journaling strip. The top, right and left edges of the sleeve are taped to the background page to form a channel for the journaling.

Adventures in Journaling

 Moving Pages

Pop Open an Umbrella

 **SUPPLIES**

Paper Adventures paper, including Dee-lightful Prints in Bumbling Bees Sunflower and Heavenly Hearts Rose, Jill's Paper Doll World SceneMakers in Clear Sky, Two-Tone Archivals in Orange Sherbet, Flannel Sheets in Sugar, and Mix'n'Match Archivals Classic Collection in Sugar Solid. Brass plated fasteners from office supply store. Self-Stick Lettering by Paper Adventures in Sugar. Matting around page title by Magic Matter.

HOT SHOT—What happens when a child shows both her tender and her playful sides? What environment brings out a child's malleable nature? How does she express herself?

DESIGN TIPS:

1) Tucking the bottom photos into the "sand" adds a three-dimensional sense to the page.

2) Before I mat a photo with color, I check to see if a thin white mat would be desirable. Usually the thin white mat brightens up the photo and gives the picture more definition.

 **TAKE NOTE**

Taking a Shot at Poetry
I outlined the journaling space on a piece of paper and asked Daniele to write her story for me. Then I traced her penciled writing with the aid of my light box.

ADAPT THIS PAGE:
You could make a similar umbrella for a rainy day page. I reinforced the holes under the fasteners with a see-through Avery hole reinforcement sticker.

 **LOOK FURTHER**

Bold and Beautiful
Again, one simple embellishment ties a gallery of photos together. Be big and bold when you create backgrounds for your pages or your layouts may look cluttered.

Pull-Out Journaling

SUPPLIES

Paper Adventures paper, including k.p. kids & co. in Lotsa-dots; Two-Tone Archivals in Mercury, Cardinal and Banana Split; and Mix'n'Match Archivals Classic Collection in Sugar Solid. Self-Stick Lettering by Paper Adventures in Ruby.

Remembering Together

We sat together and scribbled out a list of Michael's memorable winnings. Not only was I gleaning valuable information that I could journal as a list, but we also had a great time remembering Michael's successes.

ADAPT THIS PAGE:

1) Put a pocket behind a photo and slip your journaling in the pocket.

2) String your page title words together with a bit of twine or hemp.

KING OF THE CLAW—What arcade games do your family members like to play? What are they good at? How did they get started?

DESIGN TIP: This squirrelly piece of plastic twine was lying on the ground outside my house. I walked past it twice and then thought, "Hmm. Looks interesting. Good color." My husband tried to toss it out twice. Part of designing a fun page is thinking out of the box. Trash is definitely "out of the box."

Seeing Patterns in Photos

The jumble of brightly colored dots in the patterned paper mimics the jumble of toys inside "the claw." Try looking at your photos and your paper through squinted eyes. When we remove hard edges, our creative self is free to make new associations.

Adventures in Journaling 37

Chasing Great Tales

SUPPLIES

Paper Adventures paper, including k.p. kids & co. in Blue Gingham Daisy, Two-Tone Archivals in Grape and Grasshopper, and Mix'n'Match Archivals Classic Collection in Neptune Solid and Sugar Solid. Self-Stick Lettering by Paper Adventures in Grape. Brass plated fasteners from office supply store. D-ring from Dyas. Matting around page title by Magic Matter from PuzzleMates.

<u>Puppy Love</u>—What has cheered you immensely? Who sends you photos over the Internet and why? What was your response?

Design Tip: Big images allow you to use big bold prints. My rule is the print can't be larger than the head of my photographed subject.

<u>Adapt This Page:</u>

1) The pull strap on the journaling is made like the buckle end of a leather belt. Then the fastener passes through the folded ends to secure them around the D-ring. You could use a similar pull-strap on any pull out journaling.

2) Big picture, big design. The journaling is tucked away so it doesn't interfere. Copy this idea by creating a pocket behind your photo.

Imaginary Friends

To tell the story of how this e-mailed photo affected us, I wrote an imaginary response to the breeder. When you are unsure of what to write, imagine that you are writing a letter to a friend. Envisioning the reader helps you be a better writer.

Carte Blanche on Color

Usually you pick up color cues from your photos, but when the photo is all white, the colors are up to you. I chose bright and playful purple and green.

Adventures in Journaling

 Paper Piecing

Saving Stories of Our Times

Paper Adventures paper, including Mix'n'Match Archivals in Licorice, Sugar and Wedgwood Solid; Two-Tone Archivals in Brown Sugar, Orange Sherbet, Marigold, Grasshopper and Pewter; Parchlucent Paper in Sky and Mist. Calligraphy font by Creating Keepsakes.

SEPT. 11, 2001—How do you feel about your country? How do you show your patriotism? What do you appreciate about your homeland?

DESIGN TIPS:

1) Don't try to squeeze in journaling when it will mess up your page design. Instead, create a two-page layout as I did here. Then you'll have lots of room to journal and give all your page elements the attention they deserve.

2) I was inspired by a photo from a news magazine to create this page. I traced the central elements of the photo to make my paper piecing. Then I referred to the original for details such as the draping of Lady Liberty's gown.

Expressive Writing

I wrote this prose a couple of weeks after the tragedy. Your scrapbook is the perfect place to put your literary efforts. Families and friends will most appreciate what you have to say.

Tieing Together Feelings

The Parchlucent mat behind the photo of the newspaper poster and around my photo recalls the surreal feeling of that horrible day and following weeks.

ADAPT THIS PAGE:

The right hand page layout could work with any poem at the top of the page and any two photos below. The left hand page layout seems to me to be an important reminder that she still stands. God bless America.

Adventures in Journaling 39

Cherry & Cheery Checks

<u>Seeing Red</u>—What should you examine with fresh eyes? What do you take for granted? What common sights might surprise a foreign visitor?

<u>Design Tips</u>:

1) Big images allow you to use big bold prints. My rule is the print can't be larger than the head of my photographed subject.

2) Notice how the plaid corners on the journaling boxes extend into the mat? Before gluing them down, I lined them up with the corners and also tried them this way. This way looked best. The point? Play first, glue second.

<u>Adapt This Page</u>:

No photo? No problem. With a dramatic paper-piecing element as an illustration, you can journal any story regardless of whether you have a snapshot as an accompaniment.

Let the Colors Pour in
Starting right now, really look at the world around you. What items are similar in color? In shape? In size? What's different? Ask yourself this creative question, "What is this like?" The answer will surprise you and awaken your creative juices.

Paper Adventures paper, including Two-Tone Archivals in Cardinal and Flannel; Mix'n'Match Archivals Classic Collection in Licorice Solid, Sugar Solid, Ruby Plaid and Ruby Solid; Velveteen Paper in Licorice; and k.p. kids & co. in Red Simply Gingham. Lettering font by Creating Keepsakes.

Red Roving
In the big journaling box, the word RED is…RED. Changing the color of the words is fun. The writing is purposely repetitive to build up a rhythm. Borrow the style of this paragraph and try your hand at writing about similar items in your world.

40 Adventures in Journaling

Teaming Up for Fun

SUPPLIES

Paper by Paper Adventures, including Two-Tone Archivals in Cardinal, Parchlucent Prints Paper in Sugar Stars; Diamond Dust in Daffodil; and Mix'n'Match Archivals Classic Collection in Navy Polkadots, Sugar Solid and Navy Solid. Brass-plated fasteners from office supply store.

Positive Messages

I keep a little notebook in my purse. The Globetrotters had special sessions for parents to keep us up to speed on what they were trying to teach our kids. The comments from the individual Globetrotters were delightful, so I took notes that I later used in my journaling.

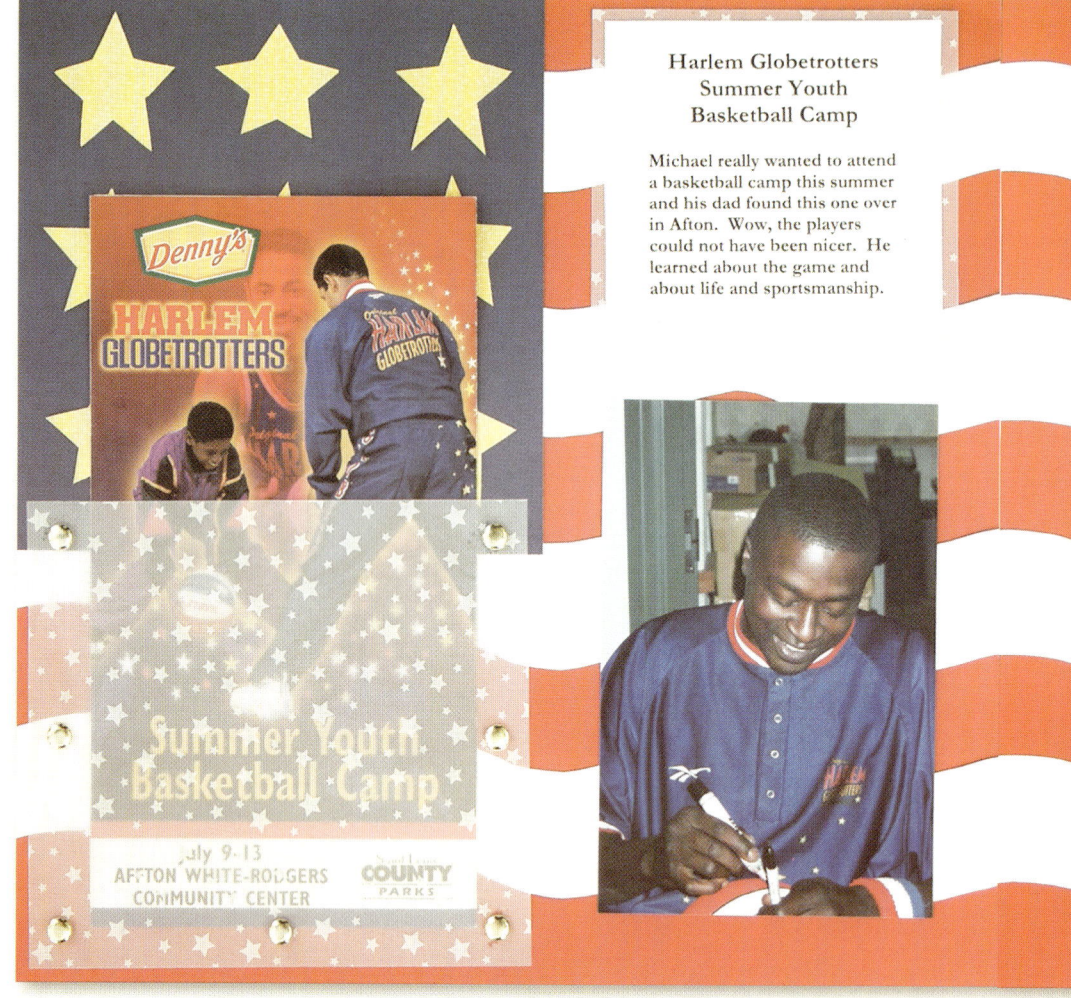

Harlem Globetrotters Summer Youth Basketball Camp

Michael really wanted to attend a basketball camp this summer and his dad found this one over in Afton. Wow, the players could not have been nicer. He learned about the game and about life and sportsmanship.

HARLEM GLOBETROTTERS—How do you teach your children good values? Who has helped you teach those values? What activities bring those values home?

DESIGN TIPS:

1) One of the keys to paper piecing is to simplify. Our flag has a lot more stars than this one does, but there are enough stars here to make the point.

2) See how the yellow stars are repeated as white stars in the Parchlucent? And how those same stars reappear on the Globetrotters' jerseys? Another page that repeats simple shapes is the Grandpa Claus (page 20). On that page, the round berries are repeated in the Parchlucent Polkadots and in the dots in the Jill's Paper Doll World MatchMakers Geranium Weave. Simple repetition strengthens your pages.

ADAPT THIS PAGE:

This paper-piecing pattern of stars and stripes would work well for any patriotic event.

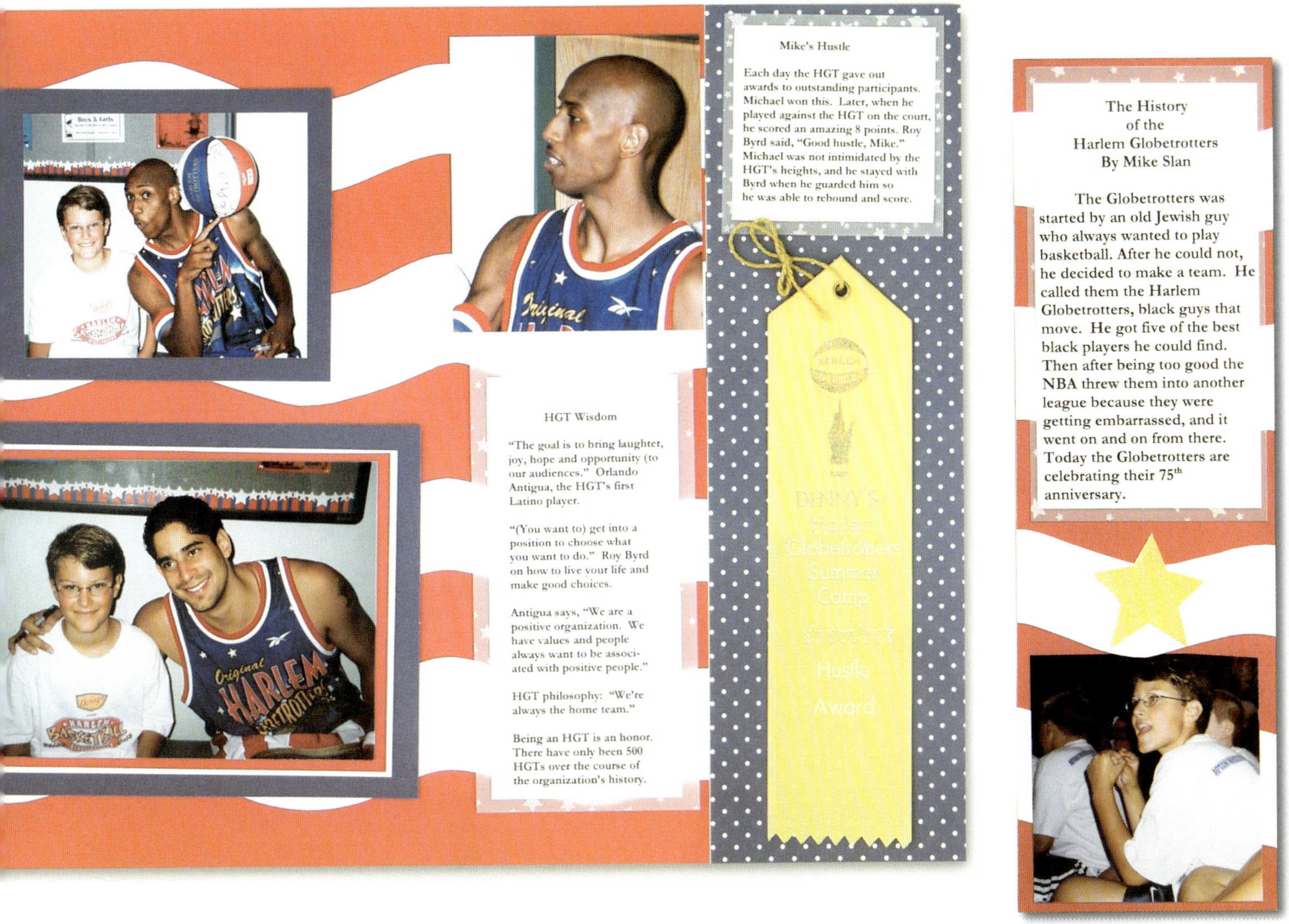

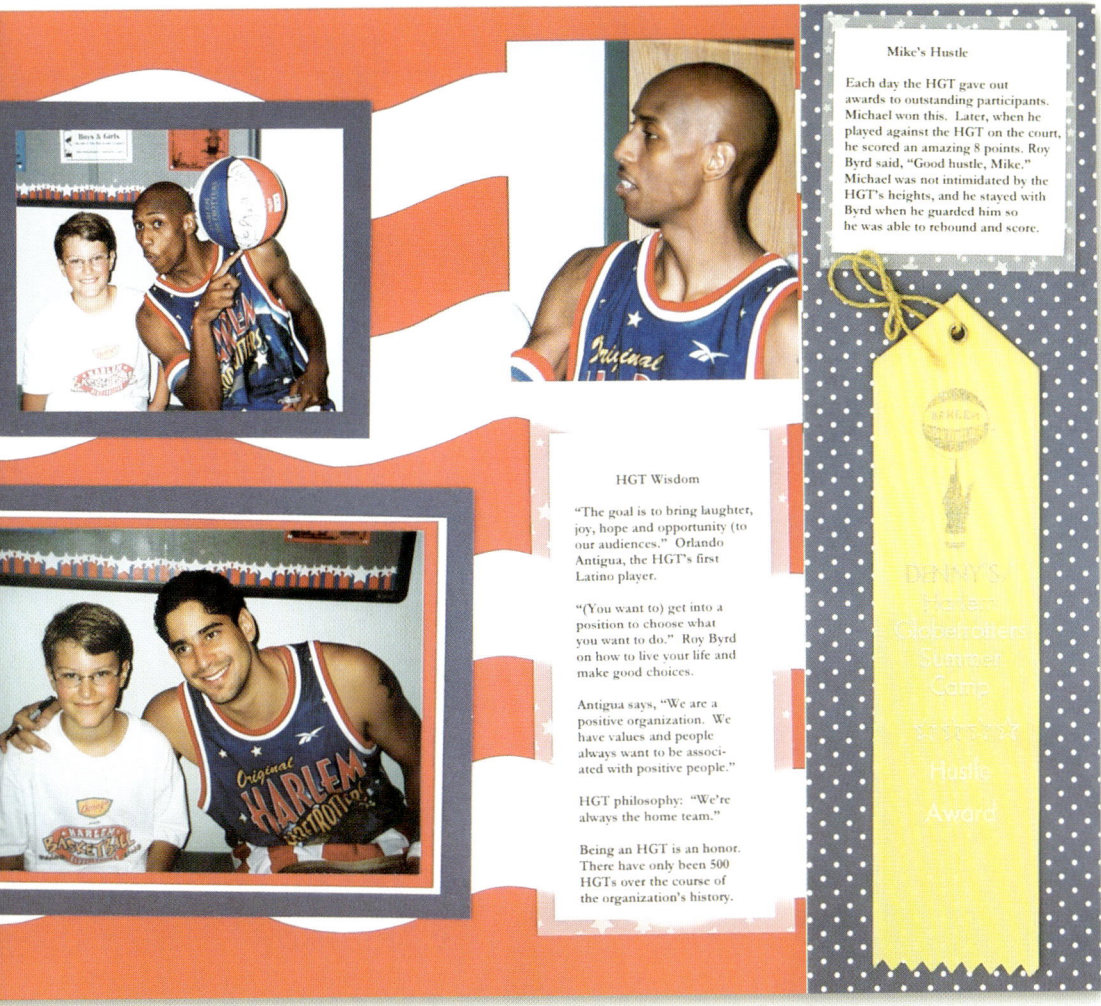

Mike's Hustle
Each day the HGT gave out awards to outstanding participants. Michael won this. Later, when he played against the HGT on the court, he scored an amazing 8 points. Roy Byrd said, "Good hustle, Mike." Michael was not intimidated by the HGT's heights, and he stayed with Byrd when he guarded him so he was able to rebound and score.
HGT Wisdom
"The goal is to bring laughter, joy, hope and opportunity (to our audiences." Orlando Antigua, the HGT's first Latino player.
"(You want to) get into a position to choose what you want to do." Roy Byrd on how to live your life and make good choices.
Antigua says, "We are a positive organization. We have values and people always want to be associated with positive people."
HGT philosophy: "We're always the home team."
Being an HGT is an honor. There have only been 500 HGTs over the course of the organization's history.
Harlem Globetrotters Summer Camp
Hustle Award
The History of the Harlem Globetrotters By Mike Slan
The Globetrotters was started by an old Jewish guy who always wanted to play basketball. After he could not, he decided to make a team. He called them the Harlem Globetrotters, black guys that move. He got five of the best black players he could find. Then after being too good the NBA threw them into another league because they were getting embarrassed, and it went on and on from there. Today the Globetrotters are celebrating their 75th anniversary.
Original Harlem Globetrotters

DESIGN TIP: I must have taken four rolls of film with three cameras to get these shots. When you have a tricky lighting situation (as I did with the gymnasium where the camp was held), try several cameras and film speeds. Often you won't know what has worked until after the pictures come back from the developer.

TAKE NOTE

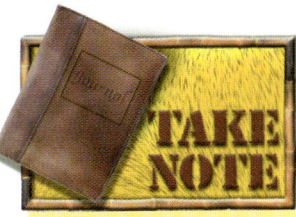

Points of View

I asked Michael to retell the history of the Globetrotters in his own words (see flap above). Ask your child to tell his version of a story. Include that as part of your journaling.

LOOK FURTHER

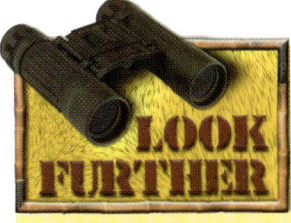

Mixed Memorabilia

Not only is there a lot of information and pictures on this spread, but I also managed to save a brochure and a ribbon. Adding the Page Flipper gave me another 6" x 12" of usable space. I could have gone to several pages, but this layout is more dramatic.

42   Adventures in Journaling

A Garden of Paper Delight

SUPPLIES

Paper Adventures paper, including Two-Tone Archivals in Jasper, Spruce, Forest, Emerald, Blue Jay, Pewter, Mercury, Marigold, Tutti Frutti, Lobster and Grasshopper; Mix'n'Match Archivals Classic Collection in Sugar Solid and Navy Solid; Parchlucent Paper in Sunshine, Mist and Mint.

Get Off the Mat
If your photos tend to get lost on torn-paper pages, mat the photos. They'll stand out from the background.

<u>Missouri Botanical Garden</u> —What local attraction have you recently visited? What impressed you? Why was the attraction created?

<u>Design Tips</u>:

1) The type of torn edge you get is dependent on whether you tear the paper toward you or away from you. Experiment to get the look you want.

2) Write your journaling on white paper and cover the white paper with Parchlucent for this sheer look.

Open the Door to a Theme Album

It's much easier to create an album if you start by creating a visual theme for your pages. Then you can carry that theme from page to page. Start with a title page, as I did here, to introduce your subject. Sort photos by topic or location or activity or people involved. Play with the groups to discover ways the pictures tie together.

Adventures in Journaling 43

Historical Background
Journal how this attraction came to be. Use brochures and Internet information to help you tell the story of the attraction's background.

A<small>DAPT</small> T<small>HESE</small> P<small>AGES</small>:
The torn paper pages are simple to create. By varying the colors, you can make an interesting background for any of your photos.

About the Author:

Whether your life takes you across the street or around the world, you'll appreciate the adventurous spirit of Joanna Campbell Slan, the author of four best-selling books in the *Scrapbook Storytelling* series and a well-loved *Chicken Soup for the Soul* contributor. Follow this small-town girl as she travels the world and her own backyard bringing you fresh page ideas and compelling designs. Mother, friend, aunt, explorer, and wife, you'll agree with scrapbookers who feel like they've found a new best chum in Joanna.

Other Writings by Joanna Campbell Slan

"Directory Assistance"
4th Course of Chicken Soup for the Soul

"Damaged Goods"
Chicken Soup for the Couple's Soul

"Climbing the Stairway to Heaven"
Chicken Soup for the Soul at Work

"The Scar"
Chicken Soup for a Woman's Soul, Vol. II

"And I Almost Didn't Go", "The Last of the Big, Big Spenders"
Chocolate for a Woman's Soul

"United States of Motherhood"
Chocolate for a Woman's Heart

Chicken Soup for the Expectant Mother's Soul

Books by Joanna Campbell Slan:

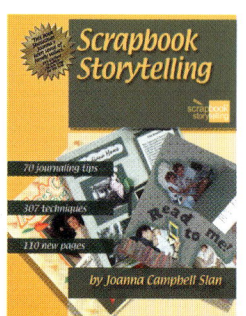 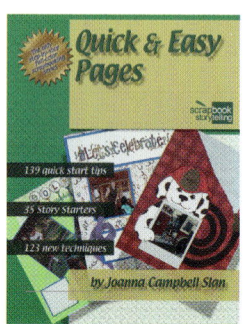 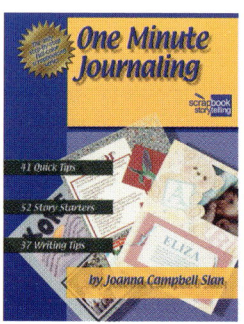 

THE SCRAPBOOK STORYTELLING SERIES:

Joanna Campbell Slan's Scrapbook Storytelling series is filled with ideas for how you can save your families' stories. *Scrapbook Storytelling* will inspire you to start saving a variety of family memories. *Quick & Easy Pages* and *One Minute Journaling* offer unique, time-saving ways to fit scrapbooking into your busy life. And *Storytelling with Rubber Stamps* will take you beyond normal scrapbooking and into a frugal crafting world of rubber stamping. To catch the latest of Joanna's adventures, see www.scrapbookstorytelling.com.

THE "BLESSED" SERIES:

Reading Joanna's books, *Bless This Mess* and *I'm Too Blessed to Be Depressed,* is like having a personal spiritual coach to guide you through life's ups and downs (while keeping your sense of humor). Each chapter includes a "Blessing" section, reminding you to be thankful for your blessings and focusing on improving the lives of you and your family.